This book is for Michael,
who had a green thumb

FIRST PRINTING
Printed in the United States of America
by The Polygraphic Company of America, Inc.
Published in Canada by Ambassador Books,
Ltd., Toronto 1, Canada
Library of Congress Catalog Number 55-5403

THE FIRST BOOK OF
GARDENING

by VIRGINIA KIRKUS

Pictures by HELENE CARTER

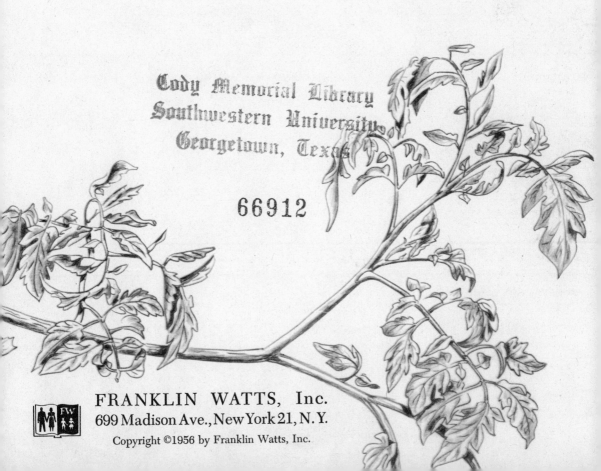

FRANKLIN WATTS, Inc.
699 Madison Ave., New York 21, N.Y.
Copyright ©1956 by Franklin Watts, Inc.

So you're going to have a garden!

Perhaps your family is moving to the country and has promised you a bit of land all your own. Or perhaps you have chosen gardens for a vacation project. Or perhaps you've just suddenly decided you want your own garden to do with as you choose. At any rate, now you are ready to start and you want to know what to do first.

Making a garden plan

When people build a house they have an architect draw a plan for the builder so that the house will turn out just the way they want it. It's the same with a garden. If you make a plan well ahead of planting time your garden will be more likely to turn out the way you want it. You won't run such a chance of finding yourself with too much of one thing and no space left for another.

So try making a "scale drawing" of your garden plot on a blackboard or a big sheet of paper. Drawing to scale is easy. You just reduce the number of feet to the same number of inches. For example, if your plot is six feet long and three feet wide, draw the back and front edges six inches long and the side edges three inches long. Now you have a garden "plan," but in inches instead of feet.

three feet wide

Dwarf Zinnias — 6 in.
Radishes and Carrots — 6 in.
Beans — 9 in.
Tomato / Pepper / Tomato — 10 in. 10 in. 10 in.
Onions — 9 in.
Lettuce — 6 in.
Dwarf Marigolds — 6 in.

Six feet long

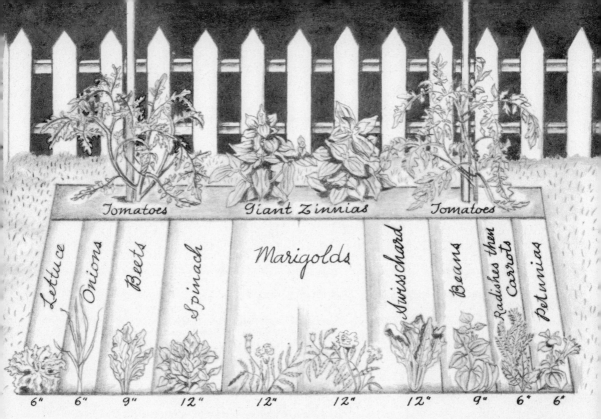

Tomatoes   Giant Zinnias   Tomatoes

Lettuce   Onions   Beets   Spinach   Marigolds   Swisschard   Beans   Radishes then Carrots   Petunias

6"   6"   9"   12"   12"   12"   12"   9"   6"   6"

3 feet wide by 8 feet long

You'd better plan to have a small garden until you know
how much you are going to like gardening. There will be
hot days when you won't feel like working at all, and days
when you would rather go off on a picnic than stay home
and pull weeds. Even a small garden needs some of your
time every week, and a garden that is too big can turn out
to be more work than fun.

If you plan an oblong garden, perhaps with a fence or
wall for background, two and one-half to three feet is wide
enough. Then you can have it as much as seven or eight

feet long. If you want a square garden, five feet square is a good size.

Whatever size you make it, you should be able to reach the center of your garden from the outside edges when you plant and care for it. If you have to work from between the rows, you may hurt your plants or pack the earth down so hard that they won't grow.

A five-foot square garden

5"	Lettuce
6"	Beets
9"	String beans
10"	African Marigolds — Tomatoes — Giant Zinnias
10"	
9"	Spinach
6"	Onions
5"	Radishes and Carrots

"Musts" for your garden

Plants need light and warmth, and the sun supplies both. So, if you have a choice of places for your garden, make it one where there is sunshine at least eight hours a day.

Plants need food, too, and good soil supplies part of it, particularly at the start. Poor soil will grow things, but it needs the help of what is called "organic matter"—manure or some form of rotted vegetable matter which is called "humus." Soil that is very sandy or full of clay does not contain enough organic matter to grow things well. Pick up a handful of your soil and squeeze it lightly. If it is too sandy, it will feel gritty and fall apart when you open your hand. If it has too much clay, it will feel powdery when dry and sticky or muddy when wet.

Growing things need moisture, too. Good soil, where water drains through and doesn't stand in puddles, helps supply moisture in the right amounts for plants.

It is best to choose fairly level ground for your plot. If the ground slopes too much, the water will run off instead of soaking down into the soil, and a hard rain will wash away the good "topsoil," or top layer of earth, where nature stores the food for your plants.

11

Now plan your crops

What kind of garden do you want? A flower garden?
A vegetable garden? Or a combination of both? Study your
scale drawing and on the margins make some notes of the
things you'd like to plant. There probably won't be room
for all the things you would like to have, but you can always
let some of them go until next year, when you may want
to plan a bigger garden.

Seed catalogs will help you

About mid-winter the big companies that grow seeds for
gardeners publish beautifully illustrated catalogs listing all
the varieties of seeds they have for sale. These catalogs will
help you a great deal when you plan your garden, for they
not only tell you what seeds you can buy, but also how and
when you should plant them, and how much space you must
allow for each kind of plant.

You will find seed catalogs advertised in garden magazines
and in the garden pages of your Sunday newspaper. If you

12

fill in and mail the coupon that is usually attached to the advertisement, the company will send you its catalog, not only this year but for years to come! If there is no coupon, write the company and say you want a catalog. Most companies send them free. A few print very handsome and elaborate ones for which they charge from twenty-five to fifty cents.

Seed catalogs are tempting, with their many photographs of beautiful flowers and vegetables. You can't plant everything in your garden, of course, and some plants are just too hard to grow anyway. So, before you order anything, find out from the descriptions in your catalog just which plants would be best for your first garden.

Look for the plants that will grow from seed planted in the spring and produce flowers or vegetables during the summer and fall. This is because you don't want to wait too long to see results, and you won't want to run the risk of having frost kill your plants before you have had a chance to enjoy them.

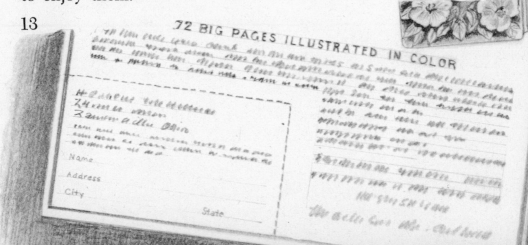

Choose plants that do not need a special kind of soil, or more sun or shade or water than they are likely to get in your garden plot.

Choose some varieties of seeds that come along early, and some that come along later, and some that will wind up the summer. Then you can pick flowers and vegetables all summer long, not just for a month or so.

You'll have a more interesting garden if you choose plants of different heights and colors. A good plan might be to choose tall flowers for the back row, low ones for the front, and vegetables for the middle rows.

Now figure how many rows your garden plot will hold. Some flowers and vegetables need more room than others. It is best to choose a few that don't take much space so that you can have more variety. Radishes and lettuce, for instance, take very little space. They come along fast, and when you have pulled them you can use the space for something else— perhaps peppers or tomatoes. These you would buy already started from a nearby seed nursery, a wayside stand, or even from some hardware or ten-cent stores. Tomatoes and peppers take quite a bit of space, but you don't need more than two or three plants of each to keep your family table supplied for the season.

Now for your flowers. Zinnias and tall marigolds take a

14

good bit of space too, but you don't need many of them to make a fine display. The new bushy petunias take only a little room.

When you have decided on your seeds, mark their places on your scale drawing. Be sure that you plan enough space between rows so that you can keep the weeds down and give your plants a chance to grow. For example, plan to leave six inches between lettuce and radish rows, twelve inches between beet and carrot rows, and fifteen to eighteen inches between the rows of beans and spinach.

Usually it is better to make the rows the short way of your plot. Then they are easier to care for, and you can have more variety too. If your plot is square, you might divide it in halves, or use the center for tomatoes and make your rows from the tomatoes to the edges.

6 inches	8 inches	12 inches	12 inches	15 to 18 inches	15 to 18 inches
lettuce	radishes	beets	carrots	spinach	beans

Now buy your seeds

You can order seeds from the company that sent you its catalog, or you can buy them in your local store. Most hardware stores, country groceries and dime stores sell seeds in small packages. But be sure that you buy *good* seeds. It is better to pay a few cents more a package than to buy cheap seeds that may not turn out as you expected, or may not even grow at all!

Most seed packages contain more seeds than you could possibly use in your own garden. If a friend is having a garden too, you might buy your seeds together and divide them. If you do this, be sure to read the instructions on the little packages and then copy them on the envelopes in which you put your share of the seeds.

16

Here are your vegetables

BEANS (bush snap beans, usually called string beans)

People grow many kinds of beans in their gardens, but for your small garden bush snap beans are probably the best kind. They don't take much room and they don't need very rich soil. Americans have known them since the days of the Indians. A good choice is the variety called Bountiful.

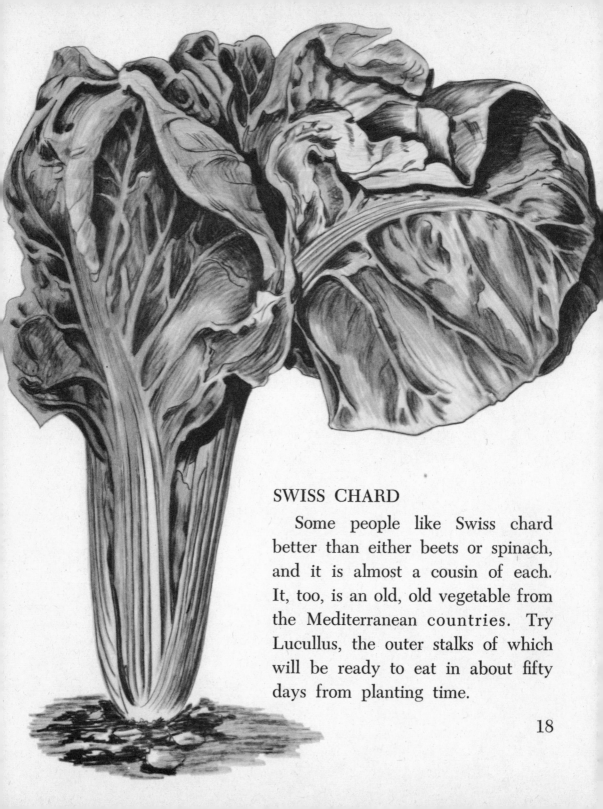

SWISS CHARD

Some people like Swiss chard better than either beets or spinach, and it is almost a cousin of each. It, too, is an old, old vegetable from the Mediterranean countries. Try Lucullus, the outer stalks of which will be ready to eat in about fifty days from planting time.

CARROTS

Carrots probably came from Asia, and people have eaten them, too, for over two thousand years. The best variety for your garden is Red Cored Chantenay, which will be ready to eat in about seventy days.

LETTUCE

Lettuce is another very old vegetable. Early Greek historians mention it in their writings. It's easy to grow if you stick to the loose-leaved kind. Black Seeded Simpson is a good, dependable variety.

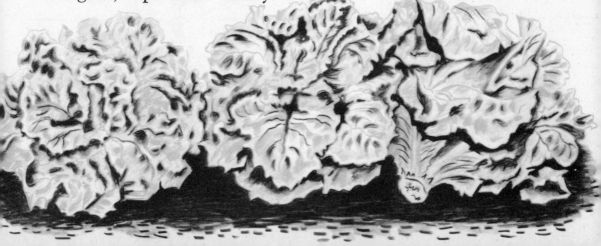

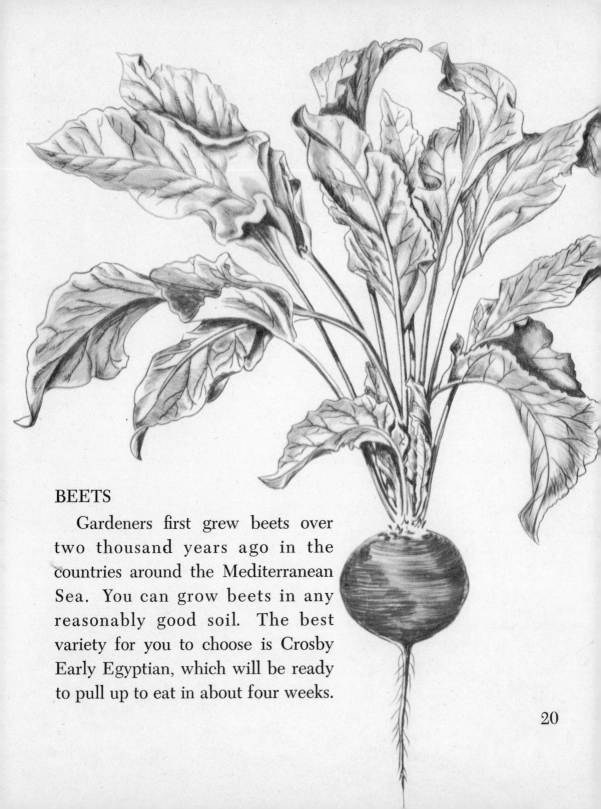

BEETS

Gardeners first grew beets over two thousand years ago in the countries around the Mediterranean Sea. You can grow beets in any reasonably good soil. The best variety for you to choose is Crosby Early Egyptian, which will be ready to pull up to eat in about four weeks.

20

SPINACH

The Persians were the first people to grow spinach. The best kind for you to plant is the New Zealand type. It grows easily and has a delicious flavor.

RADISHES

These are among the oldest vegetables in the world. They probably came from western Asia in the beginning. You can sow them very early, and have the fun of eating them in less than three weeks.

21

PEPPERS

Peppers come from South America. Columbus took some back to Europe with him when he didn't find the spices he hoped for in America. Don't try to grow peppers from seed. Buy two or three small plants. And be sure to ask for "sweet" peppers, not the "hot" ones.

TOMATOES

People in Peru were the first to use tomatoes for food. During Colonial days Americans grew them only because they were pretty. They called them "love apples," and believed they were poisonous to eat! North of Philadelphia it takes a long time to grow tomatoes from seed. It is better to buy two or three plants of the Rutgers or Marglobe variety.

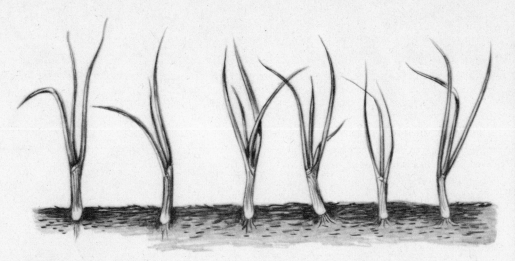

ONIONS

Buy onion "sets" instead of seed. Onion sets are tiny onions which the seedsman has grown from seed and saved for planting the following spring. It takes a long time to grow onions from seed, but if you use the onion sets, you'll soon have tender scallions (bunch onions) to eat raw, and full-sized onions in about two months.

Try these flowers

This first year you'd better plant "annuals." Annuals grow from seed, then flower and make their own seed and die within one growing season. They have to be planted every spring. Next year you may want to plant some "perennials," whose roots live over the winter and send up new tops to flower again year after year. They take longer than one season to grow from seed.

MARIGOLDS

Try to fit two types into your garden — the tall African marigolds which come in bright orange and yellow shades, and the dwarf French marigolds whose colors range from yellow to orange to red. They both bloom in about eight weeks from seed, and continue until frost.

After June 1st

May 1 to 31

April 1 to 30

March 1 to 31

Before March 1st

Climates vary in different parts of the United States, so gardens must be planted at different times. Look at this map to find the right planting time for your part of the country.

PETUNIAS

Don't get just any petunias. The seedsmen have developed
so many colors and varieties that you can choose your favorite.
"Bedding" petunias would be best for your garden because
they do not take much room. Since they are low-growing,
use them for the front of your plot. If you live where spring
comes late, you may want to buy petunia plants from your
nursery, for they take a long time to sprout in cool climates.
In warm or moderate climates they'll start blooming in about
ten weeks, and keep right on until frost.

ZINNIAS

Zinnias first came from Mexico. They grow quickly, flower fairly early, and bloom right up to frost time. There are tall, medium and dwarf types, and they come in many different colors and forms.

You'll need these tools

You won't need many tools for a small garden, but you'll want good ones. Don't buy toy tools. They break in no time. And don't buy tools that are too long or too heavy for you to work with easily. Tools come in several sizes nowadays, so you can easily find just the right ones for yourself.

First get a good straight-edge hoe. An "onion" hoe is the best size for a small garden. It has a narrow blade and is easy to handle. Then

Always carry long tools under your arm with blades or teeth down and handles almost straight up. Lay tools down with teeth or blades toward the ground

ONION HOE

SPADE

RAKE

GARDEN GLOVES

30

you'll want a spade—one that comes just above your waistline, so that you can get a good grip on it and balance it even when it is full of earth. And you'll need a steel garden rake, and a "hand cultivator"—one of those short, three- or five-pronged tools to loosen the earth between your rows. And you'll need a trowel and some garden shears and soft, strong garden twine. And buy a package of about twenty-five garden labels—small, flat sticks on which to write the names of your plants.

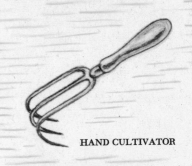

HAND CULTIVATOR

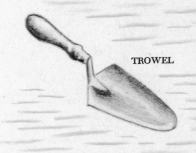

TROWEL

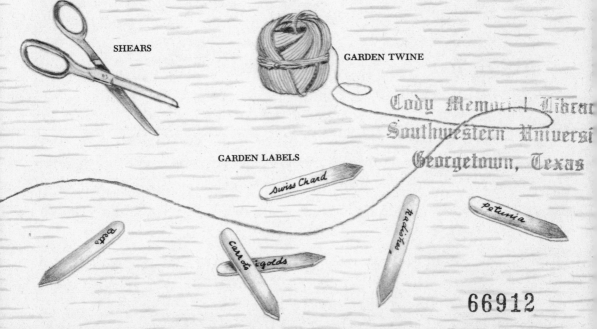

SHEARS

GARDEN TWINE

GARDEN LABELS

Swiss Chard

Beets

Marigolds

Nasturtium

Petunia

You'll need a few gadgets you can make yourself, too. There's one gadget called a "dibble," which you can make from a whittled stick. You can use it for "cultivating," or loosening the soil, for making holes and for transplanting young seedlings. Take a stick of wood thick enough to fit comfortably in your hand. Cut it eight inches long and whittle one end to a point. That's all there is to making a dibble.

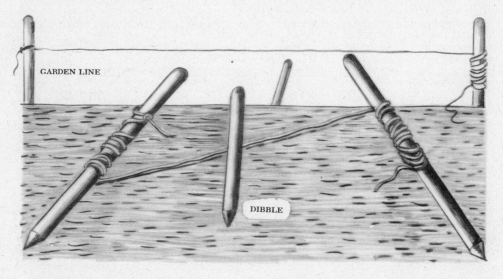

GARDEN LINE

DIBBLE

Then you can make a "garden line" to help you lay out your garden. Take two fifteen-inch stakes — an old mop handle cut in half does nicely. Sharpen one end of each stake so that you can stick it in the ground, then make grooves near the other end to hold your string in place. Now take a sturdy piece of cord, a bit longer than the long way of your garden plot, and fasten the ends of it to the stakes with slip knots so that it can be taken off. Roll the cord tight around the stakes until you are ready to use it.

Take care of your tools

Your tools will last a long time if you take good care of them. You've invested money in them, so you don't want to leave them outdoors to rust, or throw them covered with mud into a pile in the toolshed or the garage or the cellar. Ask for a corner in which to keep your garden equipment. Make a place for each tool. You can tack a strip of strong tape or leather on a board, making loops big enough to fit the handle of your hoe and rake, your cultivator and garden shears. Hang the board on the wall and slip the tools through the loops, handles down. Or you can put up long nails in pairs, far enough apart to hold the tool handles. A hand carrier made of a wooden box with two loop handles made of clothesline is a good substitute for a garden basket. In it you can keep your garden line, your trowel, your dibble, your labels, your pencil. If you have a watering can, turn it upside down when you put it away so that it will dry out and not rust. Wipe off your tools after you use them, and occasionally rub the metal parts with a greasy rag to keep them from rusting.

33

HOW TO USE GARDEN TOOLS

Follow your hoe, moving forward. Hold it about midway down the handle and lift it only a short distance from the ground. Cut into the soil with a thin slicing motion, breaking up chunks and smoothing as you go.

Hold the rake with both hands and comb the ground lightly. Don't dig in. Try using the back of the rake also to break up lumps and smooth the ground.

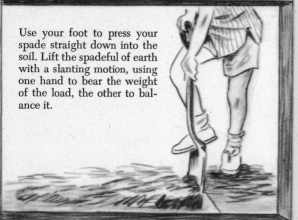

Use your foot to press your spade straight down into the soil. Lift the spadeful of earth with a slanting motion, using one hand to bear the weight of the load, the other to balance it.

Use your trowel like a big spoon to scoop out holes in which to set your pepper and tomato plants.

You'll have to kneel to use your hand cultivator. Use it like a rake, but go a little deeper into the soil to loosen it and remove weeds.

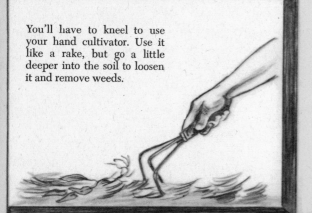

Make short chopping strokes with your dibble to loosen the ground around seedlings. Press it into the soil to make a hole for planting seedlings.

Paint handles of small tools in bright colors so that you can find them easily if you lay them down in the garden.

RAKE and HOE

TROWEL

HAND CULTIVATOR

SPADE

SHEARS

DUSTER

GARDEN LABELS

GARDEN LINE

TWINE

FERTILIZER

LIME

SPRAYER

TOOL CARRIER

WATERING CAN

HOW TO STORE GARDEN TOOLS

Feeding your garden

Even good soil needs a bit of food, or "fertilizer," as gardeners call it. Few soils contain enough of the three foods plants need in order to grow. These foods are nitrogen, which helps the plants make leaves and stems; phosphorus, which makes them vigorous and encourages the growth of flowers; potash, which helps make seed and fruit.

The best fertilizer is barnyard manure, but if you can't buy it in your neighborhood, buy some "commercial" fertilizer instead. Commercial fertilizers are made according to formulas worked out by scientists. They contain just the right foods in the right amounts for flowers and vegetables. When you see the figures "5-10-5," for example, on a package of commercial fertilizer, it means that the package contains 5 per cent nitrogen, 10 per cent phosphorus and 5 per cent potash. Four pounds of commercial fertilizer, plus a few handfuls of commercial lime, should see you through your first year. You can buy both the fertilizer and the lime in your local seed or hardware store.

NITROGEN
for leaves and stems

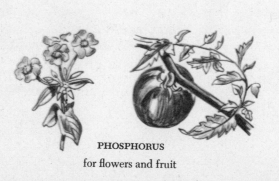

PHOSPHORUS
for flowers and fruit

POTASH
for roots

You're ready to go to work

You have your plan on paper. You have your seeds. You have your tools and fertilizer. The frost is out of the ground and you can start work. First see what condition your soil is in. Take a handful and squeeze it. Does it pack hard, like clay? Then it is too wet, and you will have to wait until it dries. Does it crumble into fine bits between your thumb and fingers? Then go ahead!

First check the measurements on your scale drawing and lay out your plot with a yardstick. Here's where the garden line comes in. Pound the stakes upright into the ground at the corners of your plot. Stretch the line from stake to stake, close enough to the ground to make sure your lines are straight.

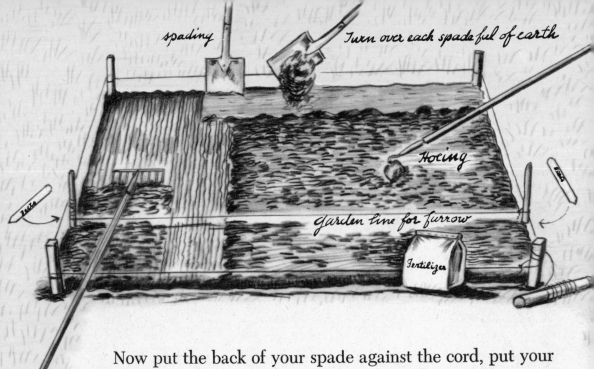

spading

Turn over each spadeful of earth

Hoeing

garden line for furrow

Fertilizer

Now put the back of your spade against the cord, put your foot on the edge of the spade, and press down. Turn over a spadeful of earth so that the top will be on the bottom for the roots of your plants to feed on. Spade up the whole plot this way, working backward so that you won't tread on the earth you have turned and pack it down. Then take your hoe, and working backward again, break up the chunks of earth. Now smooth the whole plot with your rake.

The digging has loosened the soil and let air, moisture, and heat into the ground. Your seeds will need all three. Now you can work in the commercial fertilizer. The package will tell you how much to use at one time. Just sprinkle it on top of the soil as you would put sugar on cereal, then rake it in. Let your plot settle a few days before you plant your seeds.

38

As soon as your plot has settled you can stake out your rows according to the plan on your scale drawing. Use a straight-edge ruler and your garden line. Mark the ends of the rows with your garden labels.

Planting seeds

Your rows must be straight before the seeds go in, otherwise you won't know one row from another. Take the garden line, stake each end of the row you are going to plant, draw the string taut, close to the ground, and with your dibble make a straight "furrow," or trench, along the line. If you are planting something like onion sets or tomatoes, use the corner of your hoe to make a wider furrow. The size of the furrow depends on the size of the seed. Small seeds need a very shallow furrow and a thin covering of soil. You can

dibble

small furrow for small seeds such as lettuce

make furrow with hoe handle

Medium furrow for beet seeds etc.

make furrow with hoe on edge

Large furrow for large seeds and onion sets

Mark end of each row with a garden label, the date on the top and the name of vegetable down the length of label.

plant medium-sized seeds in a deeper furrow. Plant your big seeds in a still deeper furrow and cover them with one to two inches of soil.

When your furrow is ready, open your seed packet, pour a half teaspoonful or less of the fine seed into your left palm, take a pinch between the thumb and finger of your right hand and drop it very slowly, three or four seeds to an inch, all down the length of the row. Then go back over the row and fill in where you have left uneven spaces. The big seeds you can plant one at a time, about a half-inch apart.

Cover the seeds right away, before the soil dries out. Crumble the soil very fine so that the "seedlings," or baby plants, won't have to push up through lumps. Press it firmly down over the furrow with your hand or the back of your hoe. The soil around them helps the seeds "germinate," or sprout.

Be sure to write the names of the seeds on the wooden labels you have placed at the ends of each row. Write down the date you planted them across the top blunt end, and the name of the seeds down the length of the label.

Plant the early or cool-season crops first—lettuce, radishes, carrots, beets, onions, Swiss chard, marigolds and petunias. Wait until the nights are warmer for the tender beans, New Zealand spinach, and zinnias, and for setting out pepper and tomato plants.

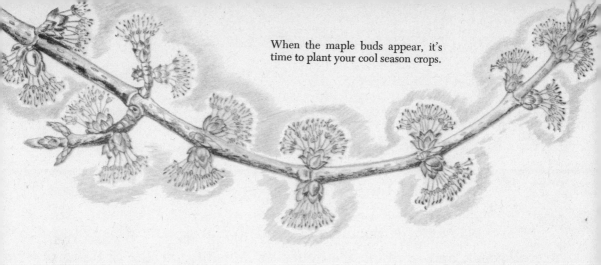

When the maple buds appear, it's time to plant your cool season crops.

Plant these early

CARROTS

Break up your soil very fine before you plant carrots. The seed is tiny and germinates slowly. Sow it as thinly as possible and cover it with a quarter-inch of soil.

LETTUCE

Lettuce seed is very fine, so plant it in a shallow furrow. Cover it with only a quarter-inch of soil.

RADISHES

Radish seeds are big. Sow them four seeds to an inch, in cool, moist weather.

BEETS

Beets like what is called a "sweet soil." Be sure yours is right by scattering a handful of wood ashes or lime and raking it in when you prepare the soil. Plant three seeds to an inch and cover them with half an inch of soil.

41

MARIGOLDS

Sow marigold seeds in a furrow about a quarter of an inch deep.

PETUNIAS

Mix two teaspoonfuls of sand to a teaspoonful of petunia seeds and sprinkle as thinly as possible on the surface of moistened—not wet—soil. Press the seeds down with your hand, and cover the row with a strip of burlap for about five days, to keep the seeds moist until they germinate.

SWISS CHARD

Make the furrow about a quarter of an inch deep for Swiss chard and sow the seed thinly.

ONION SETS

Push onion sets into the soil, flattened end down, until they are completely covered. Space them three inches apart.

NEW ZEALAND SPINACH

This spinach has horny seeds which germinate slowly. Soak them in a cup of water for about twenty-four hours before you sow them. Drain them dry on a paper towel.

Apple blossoms signal the time for planting warm weather crops.

Plant these a little later

BEANS

Plant the big bean seeds two inches deep and two inches apart.

ZINNIAS

Wait to plant zinnias until the nights are warm. Make a furrow about a quarter of an inch deep and sow the seeds half an inch apart.

43

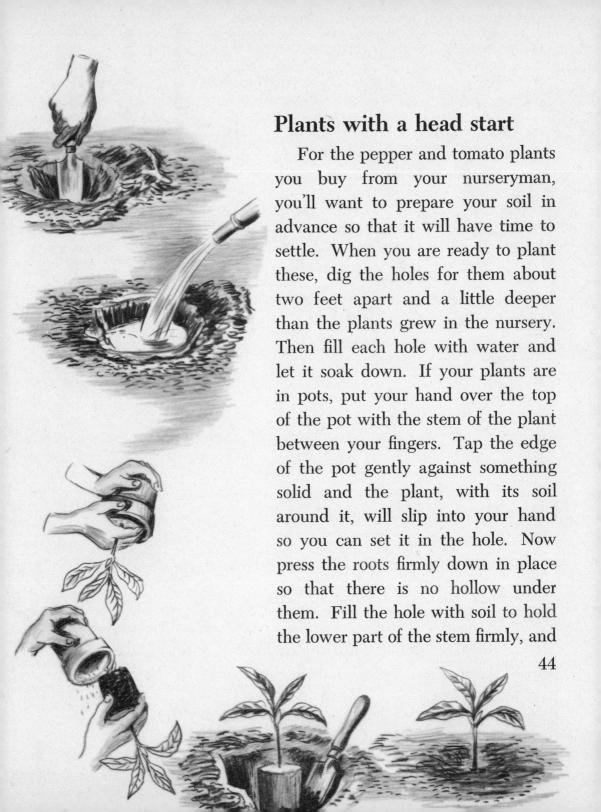

Plants with a head start

For the pepper and tomato plants you buy from your nurseryman, you'll want to prepare your soil in advance so that it will have time to settle. When you are ready to plant these, dig the holes for them about two feet apart and a little deeper than the plants grew in the nursery. Then fill each hole with water and let it soak down. If your plants are in pots, put your hand over the top of the pot with the stem of the plant between your fingers. Tap the edge of the pot gently against something solid and the plant, with its soil around it, will slip into your hand so you can set it in the hole. Now press the roots firmly down in place so that there is no hollow under them. Fill the hole with soil to hold the lower part of the stem firmly, and

44

press the soil down. If you are planting tomatoes, put three light but
strong stakes, about four feet long,
around each plant. Tie garden twine
loosely around the stalk of the plant
and firmly around the stakes to hold
the plant upright. As the plants grow,
you will have to tie the stalks higher
up. The stakes must go in at planting time to avoid disturbing the roots
later.

These rules for setting out potted
plants apply also to plants you may
buy in "flats," or wooden planting
boxes, or to any of your own seedlings you may later want to transplant. Often you can thin rows where
the plants grow too thickly by lifting
out seedlings with your dibble and
quickly transferring them to a place
where they can grow without being
crowded.

45

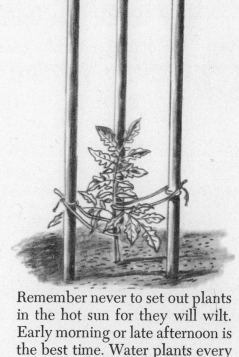

Remember never to set out plants
in the hot sun for they will wilt.
Early morning or late afternoon is
the best time. Water plants every
day until they begin to grow again.

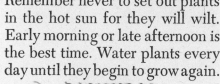

While you wait

If you could see what is happening underground, you would watch your seeds swell until they burst their outer wrappings. Then you would see them putting down "embryo" or beginning roots, and sending up tiny stems, sometimes carrying the seed coats with them. At last you would see them crack the soil above.

These hard working, tiny seeds need moisture, warmth, air and darkness to help them grow. To make sure they have moisture and air in the proper amounts, loosen the soil between the rows with your dibble whenever it becomes packed down. After a rain, loosen it again when the soil has dried out a little. This light cultivating discourages the weeds too, for it kills them while they are still small.

In ten days most of your seeds should have sprouted. Some—the radishes and lettuce—may have sprouted earlier.

46

FIRST LEAVES

RADISHES   LETTUCE   SPINACH   BEETS   CARROTS

It depends a lot on the weather. Warm weather speeds sprouting time, but cool weather slows it down.

The garden begins to grow

When your seedlings first poke through the ground they will have two little leaves. But these are not like the leaves they will have later on. They are the "first" or baby leaves. When your seedlings are a little taller they will grow a second pair of leaves, their "true" leaves. And for most plants this is the signal that now is the time to thin your rows so that the plants will not crowd each other as they grow. This is easy. Just pull one or two seedlings between each sturdy one you leave to grow. But do it gently. And always press back the earth you have disturbed. An hour or so before you thin your seedlings, sprinkle the ground lightly if it is dry so that you will not disturb the remaining seedlings too much.

47

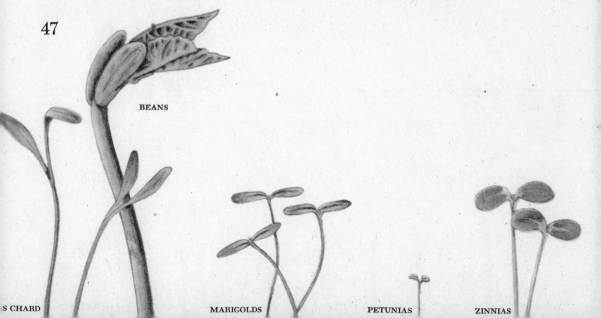

BEANS

S CHARD   MARIGOLDS   PETUNIAS   ZINNIAS

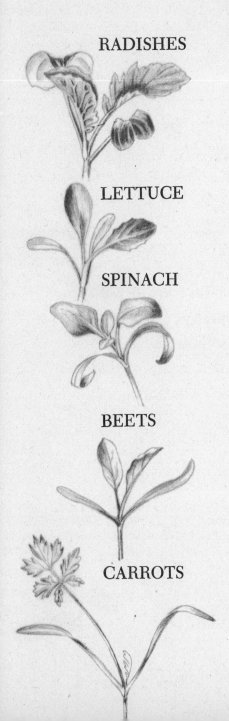

RADISHES

LETTUCE

SPINACH

BEETS

CARROTS

Thinning the rows

Thin three-quarters of an inch apart when they are two inches high.

Thin three inches apart when they are three inches high. Thin again a few days later to six inches apart.

Thin twelve inches apart when they are four inches high. When the plants bush out, cut the young tips for cooking. The plants will keep right on growing.

Thin an inch and one-half apart when they are two inches high. When the beet roots are as big as a golf ball, pull every other one to cook with the tops. Those that are left will have room to grow larger.

Thin about two inches apart when they are two inches high.

48

SWISS CHARD

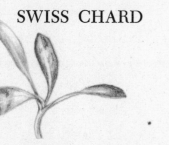

Thin three inches apart when they are three inches high, and six inches apart later.

BEANS

The little bean shoots carry the jacket of the seed up above the ground. This makes the first set of leaves. When it drops off and the second leaves appear, thin to about four inches apart.

MARIGOLDS

Thin about six inches apart for the French marigolds—twelve inches for the tall giants.

PETUNIAS

Six to eight inches apart.

ZINNIAS

Six inches for the dwarf zinnias, twelve for the giants.

To help your garden grow

When your seedlings are up, use your dibble to loosen the soil around the little plants, then firm it back around their roots. Use your hand cultivator between the rows to break up the weeds and loosen the soil so that air and moisture can get through. Do your weeding and cultivating in the morning when the sun is not too hot, and never when beans are wet.

Water your garden only if there has been no rain for a long time. If you do have to water, water enough so that the moisture gets down to the plant roots. Light or "surface" watering is harmful, especially in hot weather, for your plants send out tender roots in search of moisture, and the closer the roots come to the surface the more danger there is of their drying out when the sun shines. If you keep the top of the soil finely cultivated in dry weather, the soil moisture will not evaporate so quickly and you may not have to water at all.

Pull out the weeds before they grow tall. They steal moisture and food from your plants, and the taller they grow the more they steal. They are also "hosts" for some of the insects and diseases that harm your plants. If you pull the weeds when the ground is a little damp, you will not disturb the roots of your growing plants.

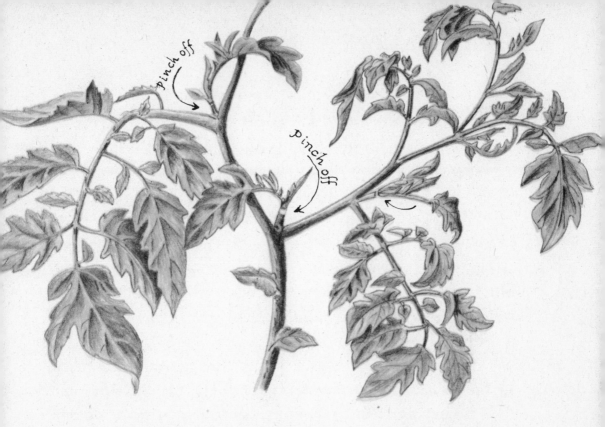

As your tomato plants grow, you can make them bear more fruit by pinching off some of the side shoots and the little soft shoots that grow in the leaf joints.

When your zinnias and marigolds are six to eight inches tall, and your petunias about four inches tall, gently pinch off the top cluster of leaves. Then you will have bushier plants with more flowers.

You may have to stake the tall marigolds and zinnias to keep them standing upright. Set the stakes a few inches away from the stalk to keep from injuring the roots, and be sure to tie the string loosely so it won't injure the stalk.

51

Help your plants fight their enemies

In your garden there are good insects, like bees and ladybugs and the praying mantis, that help protect your plants. And there are many birds that eat harmful insects, such as Japanese beetles and rose bugs and caterpillars and plant lice, or "aphids." But you will have to help the birds and the good insects destroy these enemies of your garden. Most garden enemies can be controlled with "rotenone dust," which you can buy where you bought your seeds and fertilizers. Dust it on with a "dust gun," an inexpensive tool you can buy. If you haven't a dust gun, use an old kitchen strainer, shaking the dust gently onto the plants. Rotenone dust is nonpoisonous for people and animals, and it doesn't hurt the plants.

You can pick off some of the big enemy worms by hand—the green hornworms that look like leaves and feed on tomato leaves, the soft, gray cutworms that you sometimes turn up in the soil. Don't try to use the "insecticides," or insect killers that are labeled "poisonous." They may be dangerous to people and pets and even to the birds and good insects.

52

You can protect plants from **cutworms** with heavy paper collars held together by paper clips. Push them half their height into the ground around the plants.

Rabbits and woodchucks and mice and chipmunks like to nibble juicy young greens. Even some birds will pick off the new tips of plants, and your pet ducks or chickens will help themselves. There's not much you can do about the birds, ducks and chickens, but a few mothballs sprinkled between the rows may keep small animals away.

And finally, just as people get typhoid from bacteria, and athlete's foot from fungi, and colds from viruses, plants get diseases from bacteria and fungi and viruses. Black spots, wilting and decay tell you that something is wrong with your plants. Pull out the diseased plants before they can infect the rest of your garden, and put them in the garbage pail or the incinerator for safety. Always remember that clean, weed-free plants fight most of their own enemies.

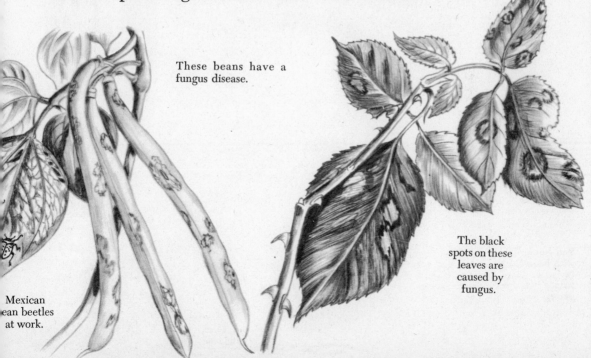

These beans have a fungus disease.

The black spots on these leaves are caused by fungus.

Mexican bean beetles at work.

GARDEN ENEMIES

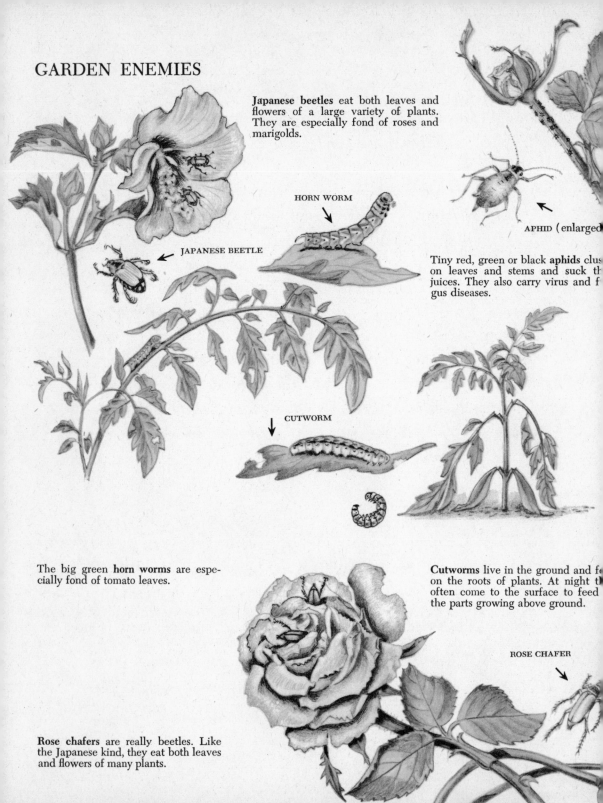

Japanese beetles eat both leaves and flowers of a large variety of plants. They are especially fond of roses and marigolds.

HORN WORM

APHID (enlarged

JAPANESE BEETLE

Tiny red, green or black **aphids** clus on leaves and stems and suck th juices. They also carry virus and f gus diseases.

CUTWORM

The big green **horn worms** are especially fond of tomato leaves.

Cutworms live in the ground and fe on the roots of plants. At night t often come to the surface to feed the parts growing above ground.

ROSE CHAFER

Rose chafers are really beetles. Like the Japanese kind, they eat both leaves and flowers of many plants.

GARDEN FRIENDS

The **bees** buzzing around your flowers won't hurt you if you don't strike at them. They are valuable because they carry from flower to flower the pollen that plants must have in order to make seeds.

BEES

You're lucky if a **praying mantis** moves into your garden. This big dragon of an insect eats hundreds of harmful insects.

PRAYING MANTIS

The little rust-colored **lady bugs** with black-spotted wings will gobble up the aphids in your garden.

LADY BUG

Harvest time!

It is harvest time whenever your crops are ready to be gathered. For radishes and lettuce, harvest time comes very early. Pull your radishes as fast as they are ready. Don't leave them in the ground to grow tough and bitter. Pull the old ones up and plant an extra row of lettuce in their place. Harvest the lettuce when the leaves are three or four inches long. Don't let it go to seed. It, too, will grow bitter.

Pull onions when the stalks are about one-half an inch through, and beets when the roots are one and one-half to two inches in diameter. Carrots can be pulled when they are a little smaller than this.

Pick beans when the pods hang long and slender, before the beans grow big inside. Chard is ready when the leaves are eight or ten inches long.

Wait until your peppers are perfectly formed and about four inches long—then go on picking them until they turn red at frost time. You can pick tomatoes before they are quite ripe. They will finish ripening on the kitchen window sill. They are still best when they are picked fully ripe from the plant, however.

As for flowers, the more you pick the more they will bloom. Cut them in the morning or the evening with shears or a sharp knife. Cut the stems as long as you can without sacrificing too many buds. Put them into a tub or deep jar of cool water before you arrange them in vases. They will keep longer that way.

Gardening in the fall

It seems a long time until spring, but actually there are lots of gardening tasks still to do. Fall is garden house-cleaning time—time to clean and put your tools away, to pull up frostbitten plants and feed your plot with some manure and lime in preparation for next year's garden. But the real fun in the fall is planting bulbs for spring flowering. Once you have planted bulbs you'll never give them up. All you have to do is plant them properly and nature does the rest. The flowers are already there in the heart of the bulbs, and next spring they'll grow and blossom even before it's time to plant seeds.

The first step in planting bulbs is to choose the right place for them. Don't plant them in your garden plot. They come up again year after year and even increase in number if you leave them in the ground. Plant them where you won't disturb them. You might pick a spot under a dogwood tree, or in front of a clump of shrubs, or perhaps close to the foundation planting around your house. Bulbs should have at least six hours of sun a day and the soil in which you plant

top of bulb

food storage layers

embryo flowers and leaves

stem

CROSS SECTION OF BULB

them must be reasonably good. If you think the soil needs to be improved, work in some humus and bone meal. Don't use manure in your bulb bed, for it could burn the bulbs.

If you have plenty of space and can spend five or six dollars, plan to plant some bulbs that come early and some that come late. You might start with about twenty-five of the smaller bulbs, like scillas and crocuses, and a dozen or so of the larger ones, like tulips and daffodils. Or you might plant some of the small, early bulbs this year and the bigger, later ones next year. Be sure to buy good bulbs, even if they cost a little more. They are worth it. Cheap or "bargain" bulbs may never bloom, even with the best of care.

Plant the small bulbs by the middle of October at the latest. You can plant them either in clumps of one kind or in beds of several kinds. For a clump of small bulbs—snow-drops, scillas, grape hyacinths and crocuses—you can make individual holes with your dibble. It is still better to dig a hole about a foot across and five inches deep. Loosen the soil at the bottom of the hole with your trowel or your dibble and then put some soil back in the hole until it is about three inches deep. Place six or seven bulbs around the inside edges and cover them with soil. Place the bulbs pointed end up, round end down.

A good rule about depth of planting is three times the

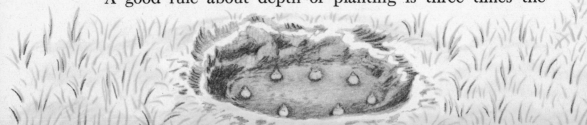

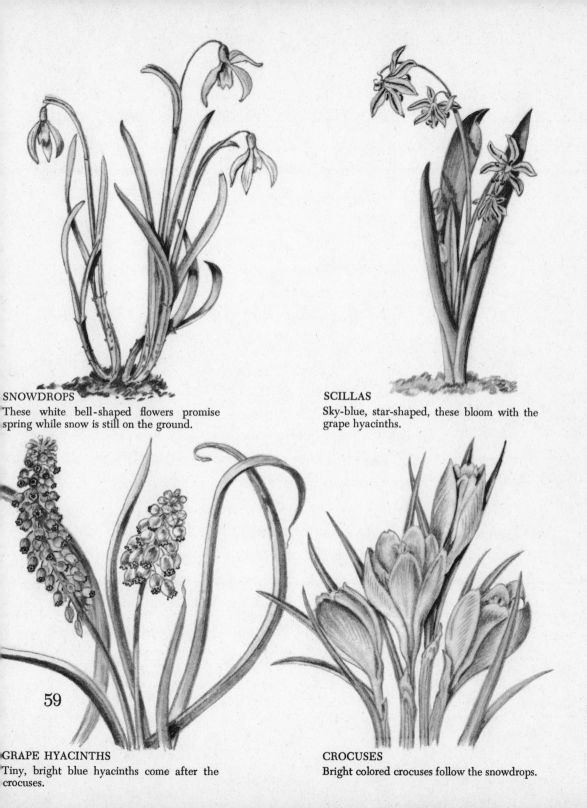

SNOWDROPS
These white bell-shaped flowers promise spring while snow is still on the ground.

SCILLAS
Sky-blue, star-shaped, these bloom with the grape hyacinths.

59

GRAPE HYACINTHS
Tiny, bright blue hyacinths come after the crocuses.

CROCUSES
Bright colored crocuses follow the snowdrops.

size of the bulb. So when you come to your daffodils, which are big bulbs, you'll find you need to dig the holes deeper. Instead of digging single holes, plant these bulbs as you did your smaller ones, but about five inches deep, with the pointed end up, round end down.

Daffodils should be in the ground by the middle of October. King Alfred and Firetail are good varieties to start with.

Six or seven inches down is the right depth to plant tulips. They, too, go pointed end up, round end down. After the ground you have planted them in is frozen, cover it with a "mulch"—a blanket of leaves or straw.

Tulips can go in the ground right up to frost time. The later you plant them the better. For your first season you might try six of the kind called Darwins and six of those called Breeders, selecting from your catalog colors that go well together.

Next spring, after your bulbs have bloomed, cut off the withered blossoms but let the leaves alone. They will look ragged but they do an important job—they feed the bulbs that are under the ground. Without the food the old leaves supply, next year's flowers will not form inside the bulbs. When the leaves turn yellow and droop, then you can pull them off.

TULIPS
Rainbow-hued tulips carry the spring garden along for several weeks.

DAFFODILS
These tall, usually bright yellow flowers open while the grape hyacinths are still in bloom.

TINY PLANTS AND MOSSES GROWING INDOORS IN A COVERED GLASS CONTAINER

Gardening in the winter

Fall planting is finished. The winter months are ahead. You can have a window garden, with pots of flowering plants and leaves. You can plant paper-white narcissus bulbs in pebbles and water in a bowl. You can—before the frost has killed growing things—plant a miniature garden of mosses and tiny ferns in a glass ball made for that purpose. And you can pore over the seed catalogs which will start coming before long. Plan your garden now, order your seeds, and then, about four or five weeks before outdoor planting time, you can do some experimenting with indoor seed planting.

You'll want, first, some "bulb pans," six-inch clay flower pots about half as high as those you usually see. You might even try small berry baskets. Whatever container you use for planting your seeds, it must have a drainage hole in the bottom. Cover the hole with broken pieces of an old flower pot, or some damp peat moss.

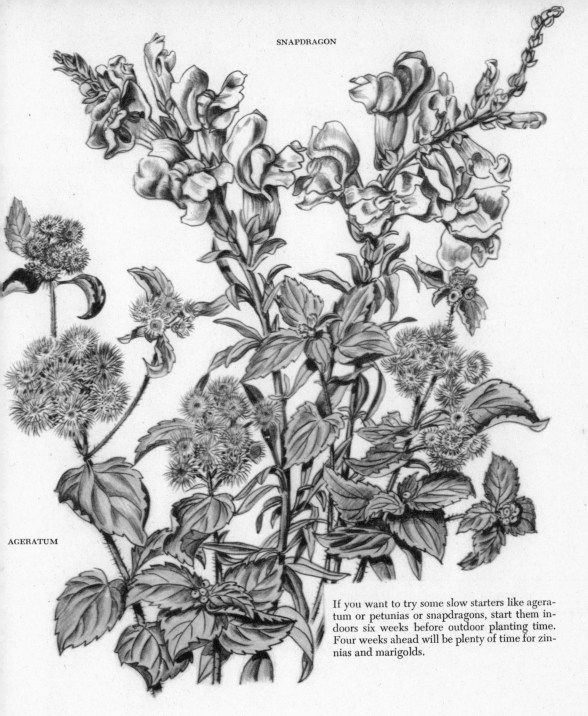

AGERATUM

If you want to try some slow starters like ageratum or petunias or snapdragons, start them indoors six weeks before outdoor planting time. Four weeks ahead will be plenty of time for zinnias and marigolds.

63

If this is your first experience with planting seeds indoors, you had better not plant them in ordinary garden soil. Garden soil sometimes contains a fungus which may make your young seedlings "damp off" and die. There's a new substance for starting seeds safely and easily. It's called "vermiculite," and you can buy it in most seed and hardware stores. Vermiculite contains no plant food, so when your seedlings get their second leaves you will have to add some liquid plant food to the water you give them. Read the directions on the box or bottle, and then double the quantity to make up for the lack of food in the vermiculite.

Vermiculite has another advantage over soil — it holds water well and dries out slowly. This is a very important thing with seeds, for they won't germinate without moisture.

When you have filled your container with vermiculite, stand it in water until the top is damp. Then take it out of the water and let it drain for an hour or so. Press the surface down with your hand and then sprinkle your seeds. Don't cover the tiny ones. Cover the big ones with a quarter of an inch of vermiculite. Now take a piece of brown paper and cover the container and place a piece of glass over the paper. There should be enough moisture to last until the seeds germinate, so don't water them again. Turn the glass every day and change the paper if it gets wet and soggy. When the seeds germinate, remove the paper and glass covering and put the seed container in the sun, but keep it in a cool room and keep the vermiculite moist. You can transplant the seedlings into your garden when they have their second pair of leaves.

It is wise to harden your plants gradually to the out-of-doors before you transplant them. First, open a window near by for a few minutes each day. When your plants get used to the open window—say after a week—take the container out of doors for a little while each day, lengthening the time as transplanting time grows nearer. And once you transplant your seedlings, keep them moist until they begin to grow. By this time your spring garden will be under way and your winter gardening will have given it a head start.

It's been fun, hasn't it?

Do you remember when you thought gardening was all work and no fun? You know better now. You've had one of the most exciting experiences in the world—watching and helping things grow. You've seen the results of your own planning and work in vegetables for your table and flowers for your house. You're a real gardener now. Probably your plans are already under way for a bigger—but not too much bigger—and a better—yes, a lot better—garden next year.

65

Some books that will smooth your garden path

*THE CHILDREN MAKE A GARDEN by Dorothy Jenkins (Doubleday)

If you feel you want a very simple book, this is a good one. It has pictures and diagrams and suggestions for a tiny garden.

THE FIRST BOOK OF PLANTS by Alice Dickinson (Watts)

The minute you start to work in a garden you will find you want to know more about the exciting world of plant life.

THE FIRST BOOK OF BUGS by Margaret Williamson (Watts)

The world of bugs and insects seems even more important when you are making your own garden.

*THE GARDENER'S FIRST YEAR by Alfred Bates (Longmans, Green)

This is to prepare you for a bigger and better garden next year.

HOW TO GROW ANNUALS by Ann Roe Robbins (Macmillan)
25 VEGETABLES ANYONE CAN GROW by Ann Roe Robbins (Crowell)

These two books will answer some of the questions your first garden raises, and will help you plan for your next one. You'll learn more about using seed catalogs, starting seeds indoors, and about plant lore and history.

GARDENING THE SMALL PLACE by William H. Clark (Little, Brown)

This will help you make a gardener out of your father or mother. And you can find some things for yourself, too.

*ADVENTURES IN GARDENING FOR BOYS AND GIRLS by M. G. Kains (Greenberg)

Do you like to try scientific experiments? Here's a book that makes gardening mean more to you.

*The books marked with a star will be hard to find in bookshops, but your public library may have them.

The FIRST BOOKS

NATURE

The FIRST BOOKS of
- BEES
- BIRDS
- BUGS
- CAVES
- CONSERVATION
- HORSES
- PLANTS
- PREHISTORIC ANIMALS
- SEA SHELLS
- SNAKES
- STONES
- TREES

SCIENCE

The FIRST BOOKS of
- ELECTRICITY
- MICROBES
- SCIENCE EXPERIMENTS
- SPACE TRAVEL
- TELEVISION
- WATER

AMERICA

The FIRST BOOKS of
- AMERICA
- HAWAII
- HOLIDAYS
- INDIANS
- NEGROES
- PRESIDENTS

PEOPLE AT WORK

The FIRST BOOKS of
- COTTON
- COWBOYS
- FIREMEN
- GLASS
- NURSES
- PRINTING
- SUPERMARKETS

GAMES, CRAFTS AND HOBBIES

The FIRST BOOKS of
- BASEBALL
- CHESS
- DOGS
- DOLLS
- FISHING
- GARDENING
- JOKES AND FUNNY THINGS
- MAGIC
- PHOTOGRAPHY
- PUPPETS
- SAILING
- STAGE COSTUME AND MAKE-UP

TRAVEL AND TRANSPORTATION

The FIRST BOOKS of
- AIRPLANES
- AUTOMOBILES
- BOATS
- BRIDGES
- ROADS
- TRAINS

PEOPLE AROUND THE WORLD

The FIRST BOOKS of
- CANADA
- ESKIMOS
- INDIA
- ISRAEL
- JAPAN
- MEXICO

NEW WORLDS TO EXPLORE

The FIRST BOOKS of
- BALLET
- JAZZ
- MUSIC
- MYTHOLOGY
- POETRY
- RHYTHMS
- WORDS

About the Author —

VIRGINIA KIRKUS was born in Pennsylvania, but she grew up in Wilmington, Delaware. After graduating from Vassar College she attended Teachers' College at Columbia University in New York City. She has taught history and English and has been an editor and a free-lance writer. For seven years Miss Kirkus was head of the children's book department of a large publishing house. Today she issues a bi-monthly report on the new books for bookstores and libraries.

About the Artist —

HELENE CARTER is one of Canada's best known illustrators. She graduated from the Ontario School of Art in Canada and then came to New York City to study at the Art Students' League. Miss Carter illustrated THE FIRST BOOK OF BEES, THE FIRST BOOK OF TREES, and THE FIRST BOOK OF PREHISTORIC ANIMALS.

———— •·• ————

● The author and the artist want to express their gratitude to the following people who helped them in gathering and authenticating the material for this book — E. L. D. Seymour, Horticultural Editor of *The American Home;* Lucy W. Clausen, Ph.D., American Museum of Natural History; Elizabeth Hall, New York Botanical Gardens; Frances Minor, Brooklyn Botanic Gardens; Clarence Lewis, The Long Island Agricultural and Technical Institute; K. E. Nordgren, W. Atlee Burpee Company; The Joseph Harris Company, Inc.; Pieters-Wheeler Seed Company; James W. Wilson, Ferry-Morse Seed Company.

———— •·• ————

● The map on pages 26 and 27 adapted from *Taylor's Encyclopedia of Gardening, 1948.*

Index